wild
WOODLANDS

BY

BARBARA TAYLOR

THE LIVING WOODLAND

Mysterious and beautiful places, the world's temperate woodlands grow in areas with moderate (or temperate) climates. They are found mainly in the northern hemisphere and include the cold coniferous (or boreal) woodlands of the far north and the warmer deciduous woodlands farther south. Temperate woodlands are very different from tropical rainforests because they are dominated by the seasons. In tropical forests, found around the Equator, it is hot and wet all year round with plenty of food available. In temperate woodlands, plants and animals have to survive constant changes in the weather, especially cold winter seasons. The trees provide food and shelter for a wide variety of birds, mammals, insects and other minibeasts. Many plants and fungi thrive in rich woodland soils. Yet huge areas of these woodlands, particularly deciduous woodlands, have been destroyed for their timber or to make way for farms, towns and cities.

WOODLAND TYPES

The two main types of temperate woodland are dark, cold coniferous woods, and warmer, lighter deciduous woods. Mixed woodlands also occur (left). Deciduous trees shed their leaves at the end of their growing season, carpeting the woodland floor with a pattern of russet, brown, gold and red. Coniferous trees keep their leaves all year round, although they do drop some leaves all year round.

AUSTRALIAN WOODLANDS

The honey possum lives in the eucalyptus woodlands of southwest and southeast Australia. Eucalyptus trees and shrubs are a rich source of nectar and pollen for animals such as this honey possum,

parrots and bats. As they feed, the plants are pollinated which makes seeds develop. The honey possum's long, thin tongue is tipped with bristles for soaking up its food.

SEASONAL SLEEP

Like a few other woodland animals, dormice survive the cold winter months by hibernating. To save energy, their body processes slow down and their hearts beat less often. A hibernating dormouse lives off fat stored in its body during the autumn when it will have eaten as much as possible. At intervals, it wakes up, is active for a few days, then goes back into hibernation. In mild winters a dormouse may wake up too often and lose too much energy.

NESTING PLACES

From tree holes and branches to piles of leaves on the ground, woodlands are full of nesting places for birds. The wood warbler builds its nest on the ground and lines it with grass to keep the eggs and chicks warm. Wood warblers migrate to temperate woodlands in spring to nest and feed, but fly to warmer African climates in the winter.

EXPERT CLIMBER

Many woodland animals are expert climbers so they can find food and places to nest, as well as escape from predators. Long, strong back legs and sharp claws enable squirrels to climb trees quickly and easily. They can climb down trees head first because their feet turn outwards at the ankle through early 180°. A bushy tail helps them to keep their balance as they leap from branch to branch.

WOODLANDS OF THE WORLD

EUCALYPTUS WOODLANDS

The eucalyptus woodlands of southeast and southwest Australia provide a unique habitat for an unusual collection of wildlife found nowhere else in the world. The tree canopy is fairly open, allowing dappled sunlight to filter through to the forest floor. The climate is seasonal, with rain falling mainly in the winter months.

Temperate woodlands grow in areas with more than 25 cm (10 inches) of rain a year and an average temperature over 10°C (50°F) in the warmest months. Coniferous forests grow in an almost continuous band across the top of North America, Europe and Asia. Temperatures are less than 0°C (32°F) for six months of the year and the growing season for plants is only one to three months long. Rainfall varies from 25-50 cm (10-20 inches) annually. Deciduous forests grow further south where temperatures are above 10°C (50°F) for six months, rainfall is over 40 cm (16 inches) and the growing season lasts from 3½ to 7 months. Mixed woodlands occur where coniferous and deciduous woodlands meet. In the southern hemisphere, the woodlands may contain unique trees, such as the monkey puzzle forests of Chile and the eucalyptus forests of Australia.

ARCTIC CIRCLE

ALASKA

NORTH AMERICA

EQUATOR

KEY
■ Coniferous (boreal) woodlands
■ Temperate forests & woodlands

DECIDUOUS WOODLANDS

About a quarter of the world's woodlands are made up of broadleaved deciduous trees, such as oak, birch, ash, beech, and maple. To grow well, these trees need at least three times as many warm days as conifers do. In Europe, they grow mainly south of the Baltic Sea with a thin easterly wedge tapering off into Russia. They also grow in the eastern middle of Asia, across China and Korea to Japan and in the middle Atlantic states of the USA.

BAMBOO FORESTS

Bamboos are giant fast-growing grasses with woody stems. They grow in forests in parts of China and Japan. Looking like tree trunks, the culms (hollow stems) often form a dense undergrowth that excludes other plants. The largest species of bamboo can grow to 40 metres (132 ft) in height. Most bamboos flower and produce seeds only after 12-120 years' growth, and then only once in a lifetime. This causes problems for animals, such as the giant panda, that rely on these forests for food and shelter.

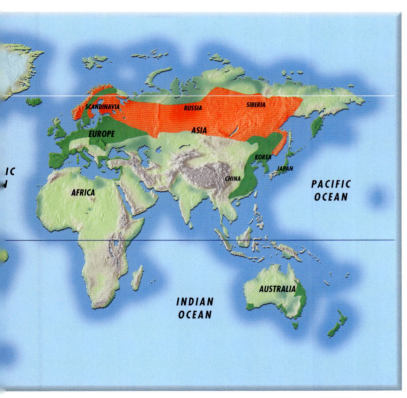

SCANDINAVIA

RUSSIA

SIBERIA

EUROPE

ASIA

KOREA

JAPAN

CHINA

AFRICA

PACIFIC OCEAN

AUSTRALIA

INDIAN OCEAN

CONIFEROUS WOODLANDS

The great coniferous forests of the northern hemisphere are the largest area of trees in the world. They are sometimes called boreal (northern) forests. From the Pacific coast of Alaska, they stretch eastwards to the Atlantic coast of North America. They continue from Scandinavia to Siberia. In Siberia, coniferous forests grow 1,200 km (746 miles) north of the Arctic circle. From one end to the other, the coniferous woodlands grow in a band some 10,000 km (6,214 miles) long and 2,000 km (1,243 miles) wide.

MONKEY PUZZLE FORESTS

The ancestors of today's monkey puzzle trees grew millions of years ago in the days of the dinosaurs. Now, they grow in the wild only in the Andes mountains of southeastern Chile. Also called Chilean pines, monkey puzzle trees grow to a height of 45 metres (150 ft). The rigid, overlapping needle-like leaves grow in spirals around stiff branches. The prickly, tangled network discourages animals from climbing the tree. Chilean woodlands are home to the Pehuenche people, who consider the trees sacred. They do not cut the trees down but gather the seeds to grind into flour.

CONIFEROUS WOODLANDS

These forests are sometimes called the taiga, after a Russian word meaning dark and mysterious woodland. The evergreen, needle-bearing trees of the taiga belong to an ancient group that produce their seeds in cones. They appeared on Earth some 300 million years ago, long before flowering plants. Coniferous trees are superb all-year-round wind deflectors, so the inside of the woodland is often sheltered from even the fiercest winter blizzards. But little light penetrates through to the forest floor and the dry layer of needles does not encourage seed germination. Only a few plants, such as ferns, mosses, and small plants can survive in the gloom beneath the trees. Fungi do well because they do not need light to grow. Wild flowers and berry bushes, such as bilberry and juniper, thrive in clearings and natural gaps in the trees. Lakes are common and form in hollows in the ground that were gouged out by glaciers during the last ice age. The ground is often waterlogged due to the low evaporation of water and slow rates of decomposition in the cold climate.

WHY NEEDLES?

Most conifers have long, thin, needle-shaped leaves on which snow does not easily settle and weigh down the branches. They contain very little sap, so there is little liquid to freeze. They tend to be dark in colour to absorb the maximum amount of heat from feeble sunshine. They don't lose much water because they have a waxy surface and only a few breathing pores hidden in the bottom of grooves along the length of the needles. Reducing water loss is important because roots cannot absorb water when the soil is frozen.

WINTER SURVIVAL

During winter, some animals from the cold Arctic and tundra lands migrate south to shelter in conifer forests. Packs of wolves may follow their prey, reindeer or caribou, into the forests. Forest residents such as woodchucks and bats hibernate through the winter, while bears doze to save energy. Many birds migrate south to warmer climates and return in spring.

FEEDING ON CONES

The tough, waxy needles of conifers are difficult to eat and most animals leave them alone. But the seeds in their cones are a vital source of nourishment. The crossbill has an extraordinary crossed beak to help it prise and lever the protein-rich seeds from cones. It may collect as many as a thousand seeds a day. A bigger bird called a nutcracker can crush cones with a straightforward bite to release the seeds.

TREE SHAPES

Firs and spruces, such as these Colorado spruces, are shaped like cathedral spires, while pines are like green helter-skelters. These shapes encourage snow to slide easily from their downswept branches. If the snow were to build up, the branches might break under the weight.

FIRE FORESTS

Fire is common in coniferous forests. The thick carpet of needles on the forest floor often ignites when a long, dry summer is followed by lightning strikes. Conifer trees tend to have thick, fibrous bark to resist fires. The cones of some conifers, such as giant redwoods, only release their seeds during the heat of a forest fire. Pine trees in California need the fierce heat to make their seeds germinate (sprout). Because conifers grow close together, fires spread quickly and are hard to fight. Water is sometimes dropped on to them from helicopters.

MAMMAL PREDATORS

Mammals are relatively scarce in northern forests, so predators, such as bobcats, sometimes have to cover vast distances to get food. Bobcats feed at night mainly on small rodents, such as lemmings and voles, and on birds and carrion. Their thick fur helps them to keep warm.

THE GIANT REDWOOD

Imagine walking through a forest so tall that the tree tops seem lost in the sky. Their furrowed, russet-red trunks are planted firmly in the ground and are so wide you could drive a car through a tunnel cut into them. These are the redwood trees of California, also called sequoias after the American Indian scholar and leader Sequoyah. They are the oldest living things on Earth, standing tall after 3,000 years – forty human lifetimes. Their vast size is partly due to the fertile soil and humid conditions of the west coast of North America where the trees grow in river valleys. A broad network of roots provides an enormous surface area for taking in enough moisture and nutrients to maintain a huge crown. One giant sequoia produces about 1,500-2,000 new cones a year and can still produce cones when it is thousands of years old.

THICK SKIN

Redwood trees have reddish wood at the heart of the trunk and cinnamon-red coloured bark. The bark is thicker than that of any other species of tree on Earth and helps the trees to reach great ages. Bark may grow up to 76 cm (2.5 ft) thick in places. It is soft and fibrous and a poor conductor of heat so the trees have some built-in fire protection.

SECRETIVE SNAKE

The most adaptable of the American rattlesnakes, the western diamondback is found on prairies and by streams as well as in redwood forests. In its dramatic threat display, the head and neck are raised high above the ground in a tight S-curve and the black and white tail is prominently displayed. The buzzing sound of the tail rattle is designed to frighten enemies.

EATING AND SLEEPING

American black bears are common in redwood and other North American woodlands. They are active at night, and roam long distances in search of fruit, berries, nuts, roots and honey. In autumn, they gorge themselves on fruit to store enough body fat to last them through the winter. Bears do not hibernate but sleep in dens for 20-30 weeks of the year. Cubs are born in January or February and stay in the den with their mother until spring.

RED FLYER

Roosting in redwood trees during the day, red bats emerge at night to feed on insects. This species is unique among bats in having three or four young. Most bats have only one or two young. At first, the female carries her young with her even though their combined body weight may exceed her own weight. Red bats are warm-weather visitors and migrate southward in winter.

TREE HOUSES

Carpenter ants live in colonies in the bark and dead wood of living sequoias and in stumps, logs, and dead trees. They chew tunnels through the bark with their strong mandibles (mouthparts) to make brood chambers for their young. The ground underneath a nest is usually a mass of reddish sawdust. Colony chambers may be as long as 6 metres (20 ft). The tunnels do not really damage the tree but they may allow other insects and agents of decay to enter. They also let air into the bark, which dries it out and makes it more likely to catch fire.

WHY LEAVES FALL

Deciduous trees lose their leaves to help them survive the winter.

WINTER
In winter, there is not much sunlight, and water in the ground may be frozen. Without these two vital ingredients, trees cannot photosynthesize (make food), so they shut down and become dormant.

SPRING/SUMMER
With spring rains and warmer, sunnier days, the trees come back to life. They grow new leaves and flowers.

AUTUMN
In autumn, the trees take nutrients from the leaves back into the branches and trunks. The leaves change colour as they dry up and eventually fall off the tree.

VOLE ATTACK

Many rodents live in deciduous woods, including the bank voles of Europe and the jumping mice of North America. Bank voles are good climbers and often bite off tree bark to feed on the tree's living layer just beneath it. They may damage trees when food is scarce; but the field vole is a real danger. They sometimes chew a ring of bark right around the tree, which cuts off its food and water supply and the tree dies.

LADY KILLERS

The wide, juicy leaves of deciduous trees make better meals than conifer needles and many insects and other animals eat them. But predators lurk among the leaves. Ladybirds and their larvae eat small insects such as aphids. During the Middle Ages, these beetles rid grapevines of insect pests and were dedicated to 'Our Lady', hence their common name.

NEW ARRIVALS

Young animals, such as white-tailed deer fawns, are often born in spring when there is plenty to eat. They then have the summer to grow fit and strong before winter. The fawn's spotted coat helps to camouflage it among the trees; although all deer are difficult to see in woodlands because of their brown colours and the way they move so quietly through the trees.

DECIDUOUS WOODLANDS

Warm summers, cool winters and fairly even rainfall throughout the year provide ideal conditions for deciduous trees such as oaks, beeches, chestnuts, maples and ashes. Species in North American forests are more varied than in Europe and include aspen, linden, hickory, magnolia and buckeye as well as oak, beech and maple. There is plenty of water and sunshine available in the summer months. The broad leaves of the trees spread, tier upon tier, to catch as much sunshine as possible. Deciduous forests are lighter and more open than conifer forests and more plants grow on woodland floor. Yet they are still dominated by the seasons. Spring and summer are times of plant growth and the birth of young animals. In the autumn, some trees lose their leaves and animals eat well and store food for the winter. Winter is a time of hibernation, migration, or a struggle to find food.

TREE LEAVES

Deciduous tree leaves are usually wide and flat to help them catch the Sun's light energy. The leaves combine this with carbon dioxide from the air and water from the soil to make sugars, which are food for the tree. This process is called photosynthesis.

WOODY WOODPECKER

The rapid drumming noise of a woodpecker's bill against a tree trunk as it digs out food or a nest is a characteristic sound in deciduous woods. With the sound the bird also proclaims its territory and attracts a mate. Woodpeckers have long, curved claws to cling to tree trunks and a short stiff tail that acts as a prop. Their bills are sharply pointed to chisel into tree trunks and find insects, which they lick up with a long, sticky tongue. In some species, the tongue is as long as the bird's own body.

WOODLAND PLANTS

GREEN CLIMBER

Ivy climbs up trees using special adhesive roots that sprout from the main stem. They are so fine they can grip into the tiniest crevice in bark. The ivy sticks to the tree but there is no evidence that it takes any nourishment from it. Because ivy leaves are evergreen they can photosynthesize in winter. Ivy is one of the few plants that flower in the autumn. It is pollinated by insects, such as flies and wasps, and develops blackish berry-like fruits over the winter. Birds may eat the berries in spring and help to scatter the seeds.

Deciduous woodlands grow in three layers. The tallest trees such as oak, beech, maples and limes provide the upper canopy of leaves. Holly, willows, hazel and other shorter trees and shrubs grow in the middle. At the bottom, is the herb layer of flowering plants, ferns and mosses. To survive in the shade of the bigger trees, some plants climb up them or perch on their branches to get nearer to the light. After the upper canopy of leaves has fallen, more light reaches the evergreen plants, such as holly, and they continue to grow in winter. On the woodland floor are plants with large leaves to trap light, or plants that feed on other creatures, both living and dead, so do not need light to make their own food. Coniferous woodlands tend to have two, rather than three layers of plant life because the trees cast such deep shade. The damp soils of woodlands are ideal habitats for ferns and mosses which need moisture to reproduce. Fallen leaves and dead wood build up on the forest floor and provide rich nutrients for plants to recycle. Fungi are particularly important in the recycling process.

LAYERS OF A WOODLAND

A woodland can be divided into three main layers.

THE CANOPY
The highest level is made up of mature trees

THE SHRUB
The thick shrub level is made up of bushes, shrubs and young trees

THE FIELD LAYER
A carpet of flowers, herbs, ferns, and mosses

The woodland floor is covered with decaying leaves, fungi and plant debris.

FOREST FUNGI

Unlike green plants, fungi cannot make their own food. They absorb nutrients from plant sugars or other living things, both when they are alive and after they've died. The large amount of dead and decaying material in woodlands is an ideal food source for fungi. Many of them live in partnership with the trees, taking some sugars from them but also helping the trees to absorb minerals from the soil.

SPRINGING TO LIFE

Fire in this coniferous forest has allowed more light to reach the forest floor and a yellow carpet of heartleaf arnica has spread luxuriantly. A single species of plant may grow over a large area if it reproduces vegetatively from underground stems. Many flowering plants, such as bluebells and wood sorrel, sprout rapidly in spring before the trees come into leaf and shade the woodland floor. They store food in bulbs, corms, tubers, or rhizomes under the ground, so are ready to grow quickly in spring.

NESTING ORCHID

The bird's nest orchid is named for its thick, tangled mass of roots. It grows in the thick layers of leaf litter in deciduous woodlands, especially beneath beech trees. Having no green pigment with which to photosynthesize the orchids obtains its nourishment from dead and decaying plant matter.

FERN LIFE CYCLE

Ferns produce their spores in brown sacs, called sori, on the underside of the leaves. The spores do not grow into new fern plants but into a tiny, heart-shaped structure called a prothallus which produces sperm and egg cells. A sperm cell has to swim through moisture on the surface of the prothallus to fuse with an egg cell before a new fern plant can develop. In winter, fern plants die back and their dead fronds (leaves) protect the growing tip of each plant during the most severe weather.

BIG MOUTH

These two tawny frogmouths (a type of large nightjar) are well camouflaged by day. When they keep very still and upright, their streaked and speckled feathers look like broken branches. At night, the frogmouth glides down from its perch to catch beetles, centipedes, frogs and mice in its beak. The tuft of stiff feathers at the base of the bill act like a cat's whiskers to help the bird find its way or to sense food in the dark.

EUCALYPTUS WOODLANDS

From noisy, brightly coloured birds by day, to secretive furry mammals at night, Australian eucalyptus forests are home to a variety of fascinating and unique wildlife. The air is filled with the buzzing and chirruping of insects and the sweet, powerful scents of eucalyptus leaves and acacia flowers. Dry bark hangs from the eucalyptus trunks in long curling strips. Eventually it falls to the ground and mixes with fallen leaves, making a crunchy carpet underfoot. The climate in these unusual woodlands is seasonal, with rain falling mainly in the winter months. Rainwater collects in marshy pools, creating a habitat for frogs, snakes and water birds, such as ibises, pelicans, black swans and ducks. Many birds, such as honeyeaters and lorikeets, and mammals, such as honey possums and bats, feed on the nectar and pollen in the eucalyptus trees and shrubs, such as grevilleas and banksias. Parrots use their strong bills to crack open seeds. Insects are also a plentiful source of food for other wildlife.

FURRY PARACHUTE

Webs of furry skin between the front and back legs of a sugar glider spread out like a parachute when it jumps from tree to tree. Sugar gliders can cover distances of 55 metres (180 ft) in one glide and land with a quiet plopping sound. They feed on insects, nectar, fruit and the sweet, sugary sap of wattle (acacia) and gum (eucalyptus) trees. Using their sharp front teeth they gnaw at the bark to reach the sap beneath it.

NO DRINK

The koala's name comes from an Aboriginal word meaning 'no drink' because the koala gets most of its moisture from its food and rarely drinks. Koalas only eat the leaves of certain types of eucalyptus trees. They have cheek pouches in which to store the leaves and an extra long intestine to help digest them. Koalas have claws like knives to cling to branches and long fingers and toes to help them climb.

LEAF-EATER

The brightly patterned caterpillar of the Emperor gum moth is surprisingly well camouflaged among the young leaves of the eucalyptus trees on which it feeds. The caterpillar pupates and turns into a handsome moth with eyespots on its back wings. These startle and confuse predators, such as birds, and draw attention away from the moth's vulnerable head.

STICKY TOES

With its long, thin sticky toes, White's tree frog can grip wet leaves and other slippery surfaces, such as tree trunks after rain. Their belly skin is very loose and gives them extra grip when climbing. The green skin colour blends in well with the woodland background where the frog hides during the day. At night, this frog hunts for beetles, moths and other insects, which it catches in its wide mouth.

OAK LEAF SAP

OAK LEAF APHID

GREAT TIT

SPARROWHAWK

The juicy leaves of deciduous trees provide tasty snacks for an army of insects in the summer months. Small birds rely on these insects to feed themselves and their ever-hungry young. They are, in turn, preyed upon by larger birds, such as sparrowhawks

PREDATORS AND PREY

Woodland predators come in all shapes and sizes – from tiny spiders and beetles in leaf litter to huge owls and tigers. Swooping through the trees are birds such as owls, sparrowhawks, goshawks and, in Australia, crested hawks. Among the branches are martens, Australian western quolls, and other insect-eating birds such as woodpeckers, pied flycatchers and solitary vireos. The northern shrike of coniferous woodland has a strongly hooked bill to catch frogs and grasshoppers in summer and finches and mice in winter. Larger hunters, such as the Siberian tiger, lynx, bobcat, red fox and wolverine stalk their prey on the forest floor, often patrolling large areas to find enough food. Hunting lynx range over 200 sq km (125 sq miles).

Prowling in the leaf litter are smaller hunters, such as salamanders, toads, snakes, shrews, wolf spiders, harvestmen, ground beetles and predatory fly larvae.

CRAFTY COYOTE

Coyotes eat a lot of small mammals, including squirrels, rabbits and mice. Coyotes hunt small prey alone, but work together to bring down larger animals such as deer and Rocky Mountain sheep. Two or more coyotes may chase larger prey for up to 400 metres (1,300 ft).

EIGHT-LEGGED WOLF

Although they are not social animals and do not hunt in packs like wolves, many wolf spiders do chase their prey. They detect its movement with their eyes and with sensitive hairs that pick up vibrations. A high-speed dash often ends with the spider hurling itself onto its victim. Its powerful digestive juices can liquefy small prey within minutes. Wolf spiders are sometimes cannibals because they eat members of their own species.

SUPER SWOOPERS

Woodland owls have short, rounded wings. While hunting, they sit quietly on a low perch, watching and listening for small mammals. Hearing a likely noise, they silently swoop down, swinging their feet forwards at the last moment to hit the prey, often killing it outright.

AERIAL ACROBAT

Martens leap and bound effortlessly from branch to branch in pursuit of prey such as birds and squirrels. Their bushy tails help them to balance and their large, hairy paws and sharp claws grip the branches well. Martens inspect the likely hiding places of their prey. If they find a potential meal, they kill it with a bite to the back of the neck.

BIGGEST TIGER

The world's biggest cat, the Siberian tiger hunts in the coniferous forests of northern Asia. Its enormous body and long, shaggy fur help it to conserve heat and keep warm in the snow. Like all tigers, Siberian tigers hunt alone. They stalk their prey to within 20 metres (66 ft) and then knock it over with the weight of their body or a swipe of their huge paws. A bite to the throat usually suffocates the prey. A Siberian tiger can eat over 35 kg (77 lbs) of meat in just one meal.

CONIFER WOODLAND FOOD CHAIN

FIR TREE

FUNGI

RED SQUIRREL

MARTEN

The fungi in conifer woods feed on dead and decaying trees. They are, in turn, eaten by herbivores, such as red squirrels. Carnivores, such as martens, prey on squirrels and other small animals.

DEFENCE

In the 'eat-and-be-eaten' world of woodlands, animals have developed cunning methods of survival. Some, such as grass snakes and opossums, pretend to be dead, since most predators prefer to eat living prey and leave them alone. Others are protected by sharp spines, armour or poisons. If the armour is only on an animal's back, it rolls into a tight ball to protect its soft belly. Hedgehogs, echidnas and pill bugs (a type of woodlouse) do this to deter predators. If striped skunks are threatened, they do a handstand and spray a horrible smelly liquid over their attacker. Lobster moth caterpillars may squirt formic acid at their attackers; while puss moth caterpillars have huge fake eye markings to make themselves look dangerous. Other passive methods of defence include camouflage, hiding, or running away.

CAMOUFLAGE

This *Arsenura* moth could easily be mistaken for just another fallen leaf. It even has lines along its wings that look like the veins on leaves and help to break up the outline of its body. In coniferous woodlands, many caterpillars avoid detection by closely matching the colour and shape of the pine needles.

TIGHTROPE TRICKS

At the slightest sign of danger, squirrels take to the trees, leaping gracefully from branch to branch, using their long tail as a rudder. Running up and down smooth tree trunks and balancing on the flimsiest twigs is easy for them. On the ground, squirrels often stop, sit upright and sniff the air. If they detect any possible danger, they use their tail to signal a warning to other squirrels.

DEAD OR ALIVE

When a North American opossum is under threat, it will often open its mouth and curl back its lips to reveal its 50 sharp teeth. Its other defence strategy is to 'play dead' by rolling over onto its back with its tongue hanging out. The opossum may stay in this trance-like state for hours.

SPINY COAT

Australian echidnas, or spiny anteaters rely on their sharp, spiny coat for protection. If alarmed, they often roll into a spiky ball. When disturbed in the open, they burrow straight down into all but the hardest ground, using sharp claws and great heaves of their powerful body. Echidnas are brainy, too. They perform very well in laboratory tests designed to test learning, memory, and other advanced mental processes. In some tests, they do better than cats, so may be able to use their wits to avoid danger.

BEWARE, POISON!

The brightly coloured spots and stripes of the fire salamander warn predators to leave it alone. Its skin secretes a poison that will irritate a predator's mouth and eyes, and is powerful enough to kill small mammals. The poison glands are located on the top of the head.

GLUED TO THE SPOT

Even trees have their own defence. If a conifer tree is damaged, sticky resin oozes out of the wound to seal the cut and protect the tree from attack by fungi and insects. This deer fly has been caught in the resin from a white pine tree. Insects from millions of years ago have been found perfectly preserved in amber (hardened resin).

NIGHT-TIME ANIMALS

The rich resources of woodland habitats are used 24 hours a day. As the Sun sets and most birds settle down to roost, an immense variety of night creatures emerge from their daytime hiding places. Animals come out at night to take advantage of the cool, moist night air and to avoid predators – although some predators hunt only at night. These predators have keen senses of sight, hearing and smell to find their way around and locate food. Some, such as badgers, have a special layer at the back of the eye to reflect as much light as possible into the eye. The long and sensitive whiskers of mice and other rodents are useful for feeling their way through undergrowth in the dark. Nocturnal (night-time) animals are often well camouflaged to hide themselves from danger during the day.

SILENT HUNTER

Tawny owls are hard to see during the day because their mottled brown feathers blend in well with tree bark and leaves. At night, their keen hearing and silent flight make them excellent hunters. Fluffy, comb-like fringes on the feathers deaden the sound of the owl's wingbeats. The velvety surface of the feathers muffles the sound of them brushing against each other and the air rushing between them.

NIGHT-TIME RAMBLERS

Woodlice are usually out and about at night when woodlands are damp and cool. They often climb trees in search of lichens and algae to eat. Unlike insects, woodlice do not have a waterproof cuticle (body case), so they cannot afford to lose too much water. They instinctively move away from the light and come to rest in damp, dark places.

HIDDEN MOTHS

To avoid being spotted by the many birds hunting in the woods by day, most woodland moths are well camouflaged. Their front wings resemble their daytime resting places. This *merveille du jour* moth is almost invisible when sitting on lichen-covered bark. Lappet and angleshades moths look like dead leaves. Green moths, such as the green silver lines or the emeralds, can easily hide among fresh green leaves.

BEETLE HUNTER

The greater horseshoe bat is slow and fluttering in flight and not good at catching insects in the air. It flies and feeds quite low to the ground, swooping down on beetles, such as cockchafers in spring and dor beetles later in the year. It navigates in the dark by producing high-pitched squeaks through its nose, while keeping its mouth shut. Echoes bounce back and inform the bat of the position of nearby objects and whether or not they are moving.

MASTER DIGGERS

Eurasian badgers spend most of the day underground, out of sight in their sett. They dig this network of tunnels and chambers using their strong legs and claws. At dusk, a badger emerges from its sett for a night of hunting. Badgers are especially fond of earthworms but eat a variety of insects, rabbits, carrion (creatures already dead), and fruit. Shallow holes near a sett are where a badger has dug for food, and well-worn paths trace the extent of its territory

COURTSHIP

In spring and autumn, woodlands echo with the sounds of animal courtship. Sound is a useful means of communication as they can be easily heard even when the animals are hidden among the leaves and branches. Many birds migrate to the woodlands of the northern hemisphere in spring for courtship and nesting. The beautiful birdsong that fills these woodlands in spring is designed to attract a mate or claim a territory. Feather displays are used to impress the mate, when in view. Woodpeckers even use the trees as natural drums to send messages to potential mates or rivals. In the autumn, male deer roar out a throaty challenge to their rivals and clash their antlers in spectacular fights over herds of females. They grow new antlers every year. Insects are not usually as noisy as birds or mammals, relying more on scents and colours during courtship.

FANTASTIC FAN

The male superb lyrebird of Australia has two broad, lyre-shaped tail feathers and a mass of long, silvery plumes. Having raked up a mound of soil he dances and sings on it to attract females for mating and to drive away rival males. During this courtship display, his long tail feathers spread out and arch forward in a shimmering fan shape to impress a passing female.

PANDA PARTNERS

Male and female giant pandas each live alone in the bamboo forests of southwest China. In spring, the pandas may look for a mate. When a female panda is ready to mate she lets the male panda know by leaving scent marks on logs and stones, and makes bleating and grunting noises. A male panda answers her calls and may roar to warn other males to keep away. A pair of mating pandas stay together for just a few days, then each goes its own way.

FEATHERED DRUMMER

In spring, the ruffed grouse often sits on a log and makes a drumming sound by beating his wings to and fro. The sound carries a long way through coniferous forests and helps to attract a female for mating. During his loud display, the male also spreads out his tail like a fan.

CRICKET CALLS

In the darkness of a woodland night, the male oak bush cricket repeatedly drums one of his back legs against a leaf to attract a female. He raises his wings to make the drumming sounds louder. Females (shown left) pick up the drumming sounds of the males through 'ears' on their front legs and move towards the male of their choice. Both sexes have ears but only the males can drum.

MATING MOTHS

Male *cecropia* or robin moths have lots of branches along their feathery antennae. Tiny hairs along these branches catch the scent of female *cecropia* moths from long distances away. The female gives off a mating scent at night and the male follows its trail to find her.

NESTS, EGGS & YOUNG

In a woodland, there are plenty of places to hide the young and keep them warm. Even so, there may be fierce competition for the best nesting sites. Birds sing loudly to claim the territory in which they feed and breed. Tree holes make protective nest sites for birds such as owls and woodpeckers; while other birds and squirrels prefer to build nests high in the branches. Hollow trees make ideal roosting and hibernation sites for woodland bats. Other mammals nest among tree roots or in burrows concealed by leaf litter. Some small mammals, such as lemmings, breed very quickly. One female lemming may have 30-40 young in a season and some of those young may breed when they are only 19 days old. The forest floor is alive with them in years when the weather is good and food is plentiful. The trees also swarm with caterpillars and other insect young in spring and summer, providing a welcome supply of food for hungry bird nestlings. Some insects lay their eggs inside leaves or nuts or deep inside tree trunks. Wood is not very nutritious so those that eat it take a long time to grow.

WOOD DRILL

Ichneumon flies drill holes into pine trees to lay their eggs on wood wasp larvae. After hatching, the ichneumon larvae feed on the wood wasp larvae. The female's egg-laying tube, or ovipositor, is longer than her body to reach the wood wasp larvae hidden deep inside pine trees. She is able to drill a hole 3 cm (1¼ inches) deep into solid wood in less than 20 minutes.

BABY CARRIER

Female red-necked pademelons are smaller than the males. This wallaby, found in Australia, has four teats in a pouch that opens forwards on her body. She rears a single young which stays in the pouch, suckling for about 26 weeks. It is tiny and undeveloped when it is born but is kept warm, safe, and fed inside the pouch.

CUTE CUBS

Brown bears, mate in May or June and the cubs are born 10 months later during winter. The mother gives birth in a cave, hollow tree or other sheltered spot. She and the cubs do not venture out of the den until April or June. The cubs weigh only 350 400g (12-14 lbs) when born. They have hardly any fur and are quite helpless but grow fast on their mother's rich milk. Mother and cubs stay together for 1½–4½ years. The age at which the female gives birth, the litter size and the interval between litters is controlled by the amount and quality of her diet.

VOLE CONTROL

Great grey owls feed almost entirely on voles. These small rodents tend to increase in number over a period of five or six years and then number falls catastrophically. When there are lots of voles, the well-fed owls produce bigger and bigger clutches. Eventually, they may lay seven, eight, or even nine eggs in a clutch. In years when there are few voles, great grey owls may lay only one or two eggs. If the owl's face starvation, they leave the northern forests to travel south in search of food.

CAMOUFLAGE COAT

Female wild boars give birth to a litter of up to 10 striped young in spring or early summer. The stripes help to camouflage the young so they blend into the dappled light and shade of the woodland. One or two adult sows live together with their young of various ages. Adult males live alone or in small bachelor groups that stay close to the females and their young.

LIVING TOGETHER

Living together in organized social groups is mutually beneficial to many woodland animals, such as deer, wild boar, bats and wood ants. The individuals in a group help each other to spot danger, find food and rear the young. In mammal societies, experienced adults may pass on survival skills to younger, immature members of the group. Insect societies are highly organized, with individual castes carrying out different tasks, such as gathering food or guarding the nest. Some birds, such as American red-cockaded woodpeckers, live in groups where only one pair actually nests – the others, usually younger relatives, take it in turns to guard the nest hole. They may also help to feed the young. Associations between two different living things are common in woodlands. Ambrosia beetles farm fungi in their tunnels and eat the fruiting bodies. The fungi feed on the beetle droppings, converting any undigested wood into a form the beetle can eat.

GALL MAKERS

Strange growths called galls develop on many woodland plants. Most are caused by gall wasps, but others by beetles, flies and mites which lay their eggs somewhere in leaves, buds or twigs. When the larvae hatch out, their presence stimulates the surrounding plant tissue to grow into a variety of weirdly-shaped galls. Each gall contains one or more developing larvae.

In some, the adult insect hatches out in the summer. In others, the gall turns brown and the larvae inside hibernates through the winter. There will often be other insects within the gall, some of them parasites. The oak apple gall has been known to house 75 different species of insect as well as the gall wasp grub.

LAZY CUCKOOS

The female cuckoo lays her eggs in other birds' nests, often with colours and markings to match those of the host bird. When the cuckoo chick hatches after 12 days, it quickly gets rid of the other eggs and chicks so it can have all the food its foster parents bring. The baby cuckoo manipulates each egg and chick into its hollowed-out back, hoists itself over the rim of the nest, and tips them out!

RED DEER

Red deer are sociable animals but the adult males and females live apart except during the October rut (mating season). One herd is made up of a mature female, her female relatives and their dependent young of both sexes.

Herds of adult males have a hierarchy of importance. The buck with the biggest and best antlers is the dominant male but he loses his place in the hierarchy when he casts his antlers sometime between March and June. When all the males have cast their antlers, there is no hierarchy. It is only re-established when their antlers grow again.

WOOD ANTS

Colonies of wood ants may contain from 50,000 to 500,000 ants. They range widely over trees in search of insects, such as beetles (right), to take back to their nest. A big colony can eat up to 100,000 insects and larvae in a day. The nest is made of a huge pile of pine needles, small sticks and other debris and can be 1.5 metres (5 ft) high and 3 metres (10 ft) in diameter. In the earth below it is a deep network of corridors and chambers. In most nests there are several large queen ants laying eggs, with workers cleaning and feeding the larvae. Guard ants squirt enemies with formic acid. On warm spring and summer days, clouds of winged males and females emerge from the nest. After mating, the fertilized queens fly off to found a new colony.

A SIMPLE ANTS' NEST

An entrance to the nest can be closed in cold or rainy weather, or to control nest temperature.

Rubbish chamber

Food chamber

Larvae spin cocoons and pupate inside them.

Workers move pupae around to keep them at an even temperature.

Eggs hatch into larvae. Workers clean and feed them.

Queen lays eggs.

Queen's Chamber. She is larger than the workers.

PEOPLE & WOODLANDS

FROM WOODS TO FARMS

Many woodlands in Europe and North America have been reduced to small clumps of trees in the middle of cultivated fields. Trees are slow to grow and hard to harvest. Few landowners can afford to wait 50 years or more to make money from a wood crop. Woodlands tend to survive on steeply sloping land that is unsuitable for ploughing or where people still use trees for firewood and in other traditional ways.

For thousands of years, woodlands were both feared because predatory animals lived in them, and relied on as a rich source of food and natural materials. Many traditional peoples have lived entirely from woodlands, respecting the trees and other living creatures. They took only what they needed and were themselves part of a finely balanced ecosystem. Most of these peoples now live in industrial societies and many of the woodlands have been destroyed; only traces of their ways and knowledge remain. Nowadays, woodlands provide products rather than shelter for people. Timber is harvested or grown in special plantations. Cork is harvested from the bark of cork oak trees in Mediterranean lands. It can be stripped off about every ten years without damaging the trees. Fruit and fungi are also harvested in many countries, such as France. But many of us enjoy woodlands for activities such as cycling, walking, birdwatching, and orienteering.

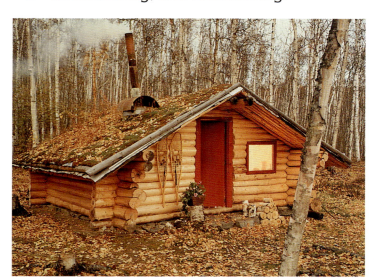

WOODEN HOUSES

Nowadays, woodlands are used mainly to provide timber for buildings and furniture. This log cabin in an American aspen forest is constructed entirely of wood, but even brick or stone houses usually have wooden frameworks and roof supports. A lot of building timber and wood for making paper is grown in renewable plantations. Fast-growing tree species are planted in straight lines to make them easier and faster to harvest. Plantations are not as rich in wildlife as natural woodlands.

TRUFFLE HUNTING

Pigs and dogs are trained to sniff out edible truffles, the fruiting bodies of a fungus that grows, in partnership with tree roots, at depths of about 30 cm (12 inches). To disperse their spores, they attract animals by producing some of the scents made by the animals. Truffles range in size from small as a pea to big as an orange, and many are considered a delicacy, especially the black Perigord truffle. The truffle industry is important in France and exports about one third of its gatherings.

WOOD TRANSPORT

Trees are bulky and difficult to move so have traditionally been transported along rivers. Areas most heavily logged were those with large rivers, and woodlands remote from rivers used to survive untouched. Pulpmills like this one are often located at the mouth of a river, especially where it enters a lake that can be used to store floating logs. Large trucks now transport logs, so woodlands far from rivers are being exploited.

TOTEM POLES

This Kwakiutl chief from Canada is wearing an eagle headdress. The Kwakiutl people built villages of wooden houses and were famous for their arts, particularly their totem poles. Carved from trees within the tribal boundaries, the poles depict animals that have a special relationship with the spirits and way of life of the community. If the tribe symbolizes an animal on the totem, then typically it will be one that the tribe will not eat or will have special reverence for. Through such symbols and spirit beliefs, many tribes express their deep relationship with the natural environment.

PROTECTING WOODLANDS

Temperate woodlands are vital to the survival of the Earth. They affect the balance of water and gases in the atmosphere, prevent soil erosion, and are home to a wide variety of wildlife. But only a fraction of Europe's original temperate woodlands remain and the great northern coniferous woodlands are disappearing fast, being cleared for timber or to make way for houses and farms. Pollution, such as acid rain, has taken its toll, particularly on the coniferous woodlands. Fires and fungus diseases also cause a lot of damage. More could be done to save the remaining temperate woodlands and use them sustainably: cork can be harvested; trees can be coppiced (cut so they grow again); new trees can be planted to replace those cut down; and pollution can be reduced to lessen the amount of acid rain.

BISON REFUGE

The great Bialowieza forest in Poland is one of the last wild woodlands left in Europe. European bison became extinct in the wild in 1919 but were re-introduced into the Bialowieza Primeval forest from zoo collections. This bison at a breeding centre in Poland will eventually be released into the forest.

FOREST FIRES

Natural forest fires in small areas are essential to trigger seed germination for some tree species, and to create open spaces where new trees can grow. But large-scale fires, often carelessly started by cigarettes or campfires, are hard to control and cause terrible destruction to trees and their associated wildlife. People who use woodlands need to be aware of the fire risk.

SAVE THE PANDA

There are probably fewer than 1,000 giant pandas left in the wild. They are difficult to breed in captivity, so this female is being artificially inseminated at a breeding centre in China. She may have one or two cubs. Pandas were more common hundreds of years ago when there were bamboo forests all over China. But they were cut down to build villages and so that rice could be grown on the land. People also hunted pandas for their skins. It is now against the law to hunt pandas. They are protected in reserves but are still an endangered species.

COPPICING

One way of harvesting timber from certain woods without felling all the trees is to cut the trees down to a stump. Several new shoots grow from the cut stump instead of one trunk and can be harvested several years later. Old coppiced trees which have not been harvested recently have several cut trunks rather than one. Hazel and sweet chestnut are suitable trees for harvesting like this. Coppiced woodlands are light and open, which encourages the growth of flowering plants on the woodland floor.

FUTURE WOODS

This hiker walking along a nature trail in a forest in the USA will gain a greater understanding of the importance of woodlands to wildlife. Our woodlands will only survive in the future if we understand more about the way they work, appreciate how and why they are threatened, and do more to preserve existing woodlands and create new ones. Creating more National Parks would preserve important areas.

ACID RAIN

Vast areas of temperate woodlands in Europe and North America are badly affected by acid rain. It contains more acid than is natural because of the huge volume of smoke and chemical fumes released into the air by motor vehicles, power stations and industry. Acid rain caused in one country is often blown by the wind over another. Trees in southern Canada are being killed by acid rain created in northern USA. Pollution from most of western Europe is killing trees in southern Norway and Sweden. Acid rain is lethal for coniferous forests which already have acid soils. By releasing aluminium into the soil, acid rain poisons tree roots.

FIND OUT MORE

Useful Addresses

To find out more about life in the forests or conservation of woodlands, here are some organizations that might be able to help.

ROYAL SOCIETY FOR THE PROTECTION OF BIRDS
The Lodge, Sandy, Bedfordshire, SG19 2DL

THE WILDLIFE TRUSTS
Freepost, DC526, Lincoln, LN5 7BR

GREENPEACE UK
Canonbury Villas, London N1 2PN

FRIENDS OF THE EARTH
26-28 Underwood Street, London, N1 7JQ

THE WOODLAND TRUST
Freepost, Grantham, Lincolnshire, NG31 6BR

WORLD WIDE FUND FOR NATURE
Panda House, Godalming, Surrey, GU7 1BR

FORESTRY COMMISSION
Information department, 231 Corstorphine Road, Edinburgh EH12 7AT

Useful Websites

WORLD WIDE FUND FOR NATURE
www.panda.org

CONSERVATION INTERNATIONAL
www.conservation.org

NATIONAL GEOGRAPHIC
www.nationalgeographic.com

REDWOODS
http://biology.fullerton.edu/courses/ biol_445/web/redwood.htm

ACKNOWLEDGEMENTS

We would like to thank: Helen Wire and Elizabeth Wiggans for their assistance. Artwork by Peter Bull Art Studio.

Copyright © 2004 ticktock Entertainment Ltd.

First published in Great Britain by ticktock Publishing Ltd., Unit 2, Orchard Business Centre, North Farm Road, Tunbridge Wells, Kent TN2 3XF, Great Britain. All rights reserved.

No part of this publication may be reproduced, stored in a retrieval system, or transmitted in any form or by any means electronic, mechanical, photocopying, recording or otherwise, without prior written permission of the copyright owner.

A CIP catalogue record for this book is available from the British Library. ISBN 1 86007 148 1 (paperback). ISBN 1 86007 170 8 (hardback).

Picture research by Image Select. Printed in China.

Picture Credits: t=top, b=bottom, c=centre, l=left, r=right, OFC=outside front cover, OBC=outside back cover, IFC=inside front cover

Image Bank; 22c. Oxford Scientific Films; 2/3ct, 3tr, 3br, 4br, 5cb, 7tl, 7cr, 8/9cb, 9tr, 9cr, 10ct, 11br, 12tl, 12/13c, 13b, 14tl, 14bl, 14/15c, 17c, 17tl, 18cb, 18/19c, 19r, 19tl, 19bl, 20l, 20/21, 21c, 21tr, 21bl, 22tl, 22/23b, 23t, 24b, 24tl, 25c, 26c, 26bl, 27tr, 29tr, 30c, 30/31ct. Planet Earth Pictures; OFC (main pic). Still Pictures; 11tr. Tony Stone; OFC (inset), OBCtr & bl, IFC & 4tl, 32 & 6/7b, 2l, 23/cb, 4br, 5cr, 5tl, 6tl, 6/7c, 6/7b, 8l, 9tl, 10l, 10/11ct, 10/11cb, 12r, 13t, 15tl 15br, 15bl, 16bl, 16/17c, 17cb, 18l & (inset), 23r, 25tr, 25b, 26/27ct, 28tl, 28bl, 28/29, 29cr, 30l, 30/31lc, 31br.

Every effort has been made to trace the copyright holders and we apologize in advance for any unintentional omissions. We would be pleased to insert the appropriate acknowledgement in any subsequent edition of this publication.

snapping-turtle guide